Insects
At
Burke Lake

A Picture Book
For Children
Of All Ages

Tommy Keith

Copyright © 2016 Tommy Keith

All images are copyrighted and were taken by Tommy Keith. Tommy lives in the **South Run** subdivision in **Fairfax Station, Va.,** which is located next to **Burke Lake Park in Fairfax County, VA**.

Images used in this book, and many others can be purchased (and you can follow Tommy) at:
www.500px.com/tommykeith

Also, follow Tommy on Instagram at:
www.instagram.com/tomkeith/

Email **tommykeith@tommykeith.com** to let us know if you want to be notified of upcoming books.

www.TommyKeith.com

ISBN-13:
978-1540595591

ISBN-10:
1540595595

We live next to the beautiful Burke Lake Park in Fairfax County, VA. I took each of these insect pictures either in my yard or while walking around Burke Lake Park.

I hope you enjoy!

Tommy Keith

Feather-Legged Fly

© 2016 tommy keith

Carolina Locusts

Red-Veined Darter Dragonfly

Wasp

© 2016 tommy keith

Zebulon Skipper Butterfly

Swallowtail Butterflies

Slender Meadow Katydid

© 2016 tommy keith

Eastern Tailed Butterfly

Widow Skimmer Dragonfly

Carpenter Bee

Cicada

© 2016 tommy keith

Gray House Fly

© 2016 Tommy Keith

Halloween Pennant Dragonfly (male)

© 2016 tommy keith

Halloween Pennant Dragonfly (female)

© 2016 tommy keith

Asian Beetle

Carpenter Bee

Ailanthus Webworm Moth

Swallowtail Butterflies

Green Sweat Bee

© 2016 tommy keith

Carpenter Bee

© 2016 tommy keith

Zebulon Skipper Butterfly

© 2016 tommy keith

Pale Clouded Yellow Butterfly

© 2016 tommy keith

Eastern Tiger Swallowtail Butterfly

© 2016 tommy keith

I hope you enjoyed looking at these pictures as much as
I enjoyed taking them and sharing them with you!

If you want me to email you about my other books and
when they will be published, just email me at

tommykeith@tommykeith.com

and I'll send you an email whenever my upcoming books
are published and available online.

tommy

ABOUT TOMMY KEITH

I love the outdoors. I am a husband, father, grandpa (they call me Poppa), Harley rider, business owner, author and photographer. I live in the **South Run** subdivision in **Fairfax Station, Va.**, which is located next to **Burke Lake Park in Fairfax County, VA**.

Images used in this book, and many others can be purchased (and you can follow me) at: **www.500px.com/tommykeith**

You can also follow me on Instagram:
https://www.instagram.com/tomkeith/

Email **tommykeith@tommykeith.com** to let me know if you want to be notified of my upcoming books.

www.TommyKeith.com

DEDICATION AND THANKS

This book is dedicated to our Grandkids, Geoffrey, Abby, James, Andrew and those still to come.

Thank you to my amazing wife, Becky, who tolerates, and at the same time, encourages my constant picture taking. Becky also helped me select the pictures and edit this book.